H E A L I N G

M U H A M M A D   A L I
T H O M A S   H A U S E R

*If you love God, you can't separate out and love only some
of His children. To be against people because they're Muslim is wrong.
To be against people because they're Christian or Jewish is wrong.
To be against people because they're black or white or yellow
or brown is wrong. Anyone who believes in One God should also believe
that all people are part of one family. People are people.
God created us all. And all people have to work to get along.*

M U H A M M A D   A L I

PRINCIPAL PHOTOGRAPHY BY

H O W A R D   B I N G H A M

CollinsPublishersSanFrancisco
A Division of HarperCollins*Publishers*

AN OPUS BOOK

Principal Photography by Howard Bingham with the exception of:
William Coupon, cover; AP/Wide World Photos, 32; Archive Photos/Express Newspapers, 64.

Healing logo copyright: Muhammad Ali, Thomas Hauser, and Four Finger Art Factory.
Healing logo design: Opus Productions Inc., David Clark, and Thomas Hauser.

First published in 1996 by Collins Publishers San Francisco,
1160 Battery Street, San Francisco, California 94111-1213

Created and produced by Opus Productions Inc.,
300 West Hastings Street, Vancouver, British Columbia, Canada V6B 1K6

Library of Congress Cataloging-in-Publication Data:
Ali, Muhammad, 1942-
    Healing: a journal of tolerance and understanding / Muhammad Ali, Thomas Hauser.
    p.   cm.
    ISBN 0-00-649189-8
    1. Conduct of life—Quotations, maxims, etc. 2. Healing—Quotations, maxims, etc. 3. Prejudices—Quotations, maxims, etc.
    I. Hauser, Thomas. II. Title
PN6084.C556A45 1996
                                                                96-9313
                                                                CIP

Printed and bound in the U.S.A.

10 9 8 7 6 5

My mother was a Baptist. She believed Jesus was the son of God, and
I don't believe that. But even though my mother had a religion different from me,
I believe that on Judgment Day my mother will be in heaven.
There are Jewish people who lead good lives; and when they die,
I believe they're going to heaven. If you're a good Muslim, if you're a good
Christian, if you're a good Jew; it doesn't matter what religion you are,
if you're a good person you'll receive God's blessing.

MUHAMMAD ALI

PREFACE

The world is adrift in a sea of hate.

This isn't a new phenomenon. Bigotry and prejudice based on religion, skin color, and national origin are an ancient dilemma. And while personal experiences and the communications revolution have made us all aware that hatred exists, not enough is being done to combat the problem. Astronauts fly to the moon. Scientists practice genetic engineering. All of us do things with computers that were once thought to be impossible. Yet despite society's technological advances, too many of us seem unable to learn the simple lessons of tolerance and understanding.

We, the authors of this book, come from very different backgrounds and lead very different lives. One of us is black; the other is white. One of us is a Muslim; the other is a Jew. One of us is the most famous person in the world; the other is largely anonymous. Yet over the years, we've forged a friendship. We respect our differences, and we respect each other.

We want to make a statement about bigotry and prejudice. We believe that most people are tired of the hating. We believe that most people are saying, "If there's a way to solve this problem, let's solve it."

This journal is part of that process. We'd like to share some of our thoughts with you, the reader of this book. Then we want you to consider the thoughts of others, which we have presented in the form of quotations at the top of the journal pages. And finally, we hope that you will add your own thoughts by writing about your personal experiences and beliefs on the blank pages.

Will this effort make a difference?

That's up to you.

MUHAMMAD ALI   THOMAS HAUSER

H E A L I N G

PREJUDICE IS JUST WHAT ITS ROOT PARTS say it is. It's prejudging; a preconceived opinion arrived at without just grounds or sufficient knowledge on which it can be based. It's the belief that members of another group are inherently bad or inferior. It cuts across racial, religious, and ethnic lines. Unlike many social ills, it's just as common in stable nuclear families as within broken homes. It's a universal problem.

Racism is deeply ingrained in most cultures. In the United States, it affects every level of society, and our racial divide is such that there are multiple layers of meaning for virtually every conversation that touches however remotely on the subject of black and white.

Religion is supposed to be a source of brotherhood and love. But religions also reflect the societies in which they exist. Thus, religion poorly understood has often been a source of division and hate. Some practitioners go so far as to claim a religious duty to commit violence, and Sunday morning may well be the most prejudiced time in America.

Throughout the world, people are mistreated on the basis of race, religion, national origin, tribal affiliation, sex, and other factors. No one is safe from this blight, and no one can claim that all of his or her associates are blameless. All races, all religions, and all groups have members who contribute to the climate of fear and hostility. In the United States at present, the focus of prejudice is on race. But there have been other times in American history when the dialogue was about employers who refused to hire Jews and restaurants where "no dogs or Irish" were allowed.

Prejudice is learned. It's not a self-winding watch. Some of the things that lead up to prejudice might be human nature, but prejudice itself is not. Babies don't know prejudice. They have to be taught. And when they are, the people who poison the well first are often a child's own parents.

Sometimes prejudice is taught in subtle, unintentional ways. A white family might be driving through an inner-city neighborhood. Suddenly, the windows are rolled up and the car doors are locked. The parents explain to their children, "This is a bad neighborhood."

> *When I was young, I followed a teaching that disrespected other people*
> *and said that white people were "devils." I was wrong.*
> *Color doesn't make a man a devil. It's the heart and soul and mind that count.*

MUHAMMAD ALI

The children look out the window, see black faces, and say to themselves, "Black is bad." But often, the lessons are more calculatingly taught.

Prejudice has many sources. It can evolve from ignorance or wilful self-interest. Often, it is born out of weakness and fear. Prejudice is a way for people to build themselves up in their own minds by tearing other people down. And it's appeal is seductive. Engendering a sense of self-worth at the expense of someone else is the easy way out. A classic example of that can be seen by looking at America's immigrant population. As despised as they might have been by some during our growth as a nation, the moment that poor white immigrants arrived at Ellis Island, they found in black Americans a class of people who it was "socially acceptable" to look down on, someone they were already "superior" to in the eyes of their new countrymen.

But prejudice is also about power. It's an instrument of control and manipulation; a tool to get the first and best of everything at the expense of those who are discriminated against. It's a business ploy, job security, a means of

getting a good apartment. It's as good as cash in most societies.

And it's wrong. It's wrong no matter who does the hating. Some people try to justify prejudice by citing institutionalized horrors. Jewish prejudice against Germans is excused because of the Holocaust. Black prejudice against whites is "permissible" because of slavery and the injustices that followed. But this "revengocide" born of group stereotypes is flawed. For if we justify one prejudice, then by definition we must embrace a logic that justifies them all.

Prejudice is painful in many ways. And for people on the receiving end, it's particularly sinister when a bigot has the power to influence what goes on in their lives. That power can be economic. It can be the power to inflict physical harm through violence. But regardless of form, prejudice backed by power deprives another person of his or her rights.

Being the victim of prejudice also lowers self-esteem. In some cases, it becomes a crutch; an overused excuse for failure. "I didn't get the job because I'm black.... I didn't get the

> *When God makes someone, the most important part is the heart and soul. What's on the outside is only decoration.*
>
> MUHAMMAD ALI

job because I'm Jewish.... I didn't get the job because I'm a woman...." On occasion, these complaints are true. Just as often, they aren't.

And invariably, being on the receiving end of prejudice spawns more prejudice. It's unfortunate when people who are discriminated against evade their own moral responsibility and adopt the view that their lack of power frees them from the obligation to act without prejudice. The one authority that oppressed people should never relinquish is their own moral authority. But often, people who are discriminated against do just that and respond in kind to prejudice.

Listen to the shrill cries that follow such an abdication of responsibility: "I'm not prejudiced; I'm just telling it like it is. That's not prejudice; that's reality.... Most street crime is committed by them. Anytime you see three or more of them walking down the street, chances are you're in for something ugly.... They don't belong here; this used to be our neighborhood.... Korean merchants are sucking the life out of our community.... Jewish rabbis suck the blood out of Christian babies.... White

doctors created AIDS.... AIDS came from black Africans having sex with monkeys.... I'm not prejudiced; I'm just telling it like it is."

Initially, it's easy to hate. For some people, being prejudiced might even be fun at first. But eventually, bigots are controlled by their own hate, and hating becomes a full-time job. It eats away at a person's insides. And it corrodes society at large.

In Bosnia, Rwanda, and many other parts of the world, the hate and conflict that come with prejudice have burgeoned out of control. In the United States, prejudice has created an increasingly large underclass that drains our resources and sense of national purpose. It causes endless misery, and threatens to undermine our most fundamental institutions, such as the right of an individual and the state to a fair trial by jury.

Yet oddly enough, it might be that prejudice and hate in the United States are on the decline. We hear a lot about racial division. And certainly, black racism is more open now than in the past, even if white racism is more disguised. But more blacks and whites in

> *Hating people because of their color is wrong.*
> *And it doesn't matter which color does the hating. It's just plain wrong.*
>
> MUHAMMAD ALI

America today relate to one another in the workplace and as friends than ever before. And these mixed racial situations are accelerating with particular vibrancy among the young, the same way that mixed ethnic and religious relationships among the youth of America accelerated a generation ago.

Thus, there is cause for optimism. And the crucial question becomes, "How can we stop the hate?"

It would be nice if we could simply vacuum the prejudice from peoples' minds, but life isn't that simple. All of us have a dark side, and bigotry is deeply ingrained in some people. Also, prejudice often comes wrapped in some very thorny issues.

Take the example of urban cab drivers. They aren't allowed to discriminate on the basis of race. That's the law. Yet it's no secret that, in many cities, cab drivers refuse to pick up black passengers. Their rationale is the "statistical probability" that they're more likely to be robbed by black people. "You wouldn't drive into a black neighborhood," these drivers tell the public. "So don't ask us to do

something that you wouldn't do yourself."

But what of the would-be passenger who can't get home that night? That person is a citizen too, with certain expectations and rights. So should society say, "Black people don't have the right to hail a cab because they're alleged to be bad security risks?" Or should we tell the cab driver — like we tell bus drivers, firefighters, and postal service employees — "You've chosen this profession and you have to perform your job, which means you can't deny service to people on the basis of race."

None of us likes to be on the receiving end of prejudice. And almost always, when it's directed at us, we think it's grossly unfair. Thus, one important step in overcoming prejudice within ourselves is to recognize the hopes and needs of others. Too often, people from different backgrounds can't imagine each other's suffering, fear, and anger. And the best way to bridge that gap is to get to know each other.

People have to sit down and talk. We have to reach out to those who are different from us, and judge them as individuals rather than on the basis of group stereotypes.

Muslims, Christians, Jews, all religions, have different ways
of worshipping God; but we're all trying to get to the same place.

MUHAMMAD ALI

Prejudice comes from being in the dark; sunlight disinfects it. And once we get to know people who are different, we might still dislike some of them. But it will be for their individual characteristics; not for their religion or the color of their skin.

"You don't know me! How can you hate me?"

That's the question each of us has the right to ask when we're prejudged by someone else. Brotherhood begins with one-on-one relationships. And while some people might promote tolerance on the basis that "all of us are the same," we prefer the view that all people are different from each other. That means all white people are different from each other. All black people are different from each other. All Muslims are different from each other. All Christians are different from each other. All Jews are different from each other. All Buddhists are different from each other. All Italians are different from each other. All Iraqis are different from each other.

These differences mean that each of us should view every other person as an individual based on his or her own merits. And once we do that, the next step is for all of us to find common ground.

The great monotheistic religions of the world all worship the same God. They just call Him by different names.

Jews and Muslims lived in harmony for centuries. Indeed, the prophet Muhammad referred to Jews as "People of the Book," and the Qur'an recognizes Abraham, Isaac, Jacob, Moses, and many others from the Old Testament as prophets.

In the American civil rights movement, there has been a long working relationship between black and white.

Moreover, when people are forced to interact to survive, their prejudices diminish. That's evident in the military during combat. And people who are pushed together in other interdependent situations, such as sports teams in pursuit of victory, cooperate in pursuit of a common goal.

Common ground and common goals also demand common treatment. Thus, while each of us has the right to condemn improper

> *If I hated, I couldn't think. If I hated, I couldn't eat.*
> *If I hated, I couldn't work. I'd be nervous; I'd be frustrated. I don't hate.*
>
> MUHAMMAD ALI

behavior by people with beliefs different from our own, it's important that we hold "our own kind" to the same standards that we hold others. Condoning misdeeds simply because the perpetrator is of our own race or religion is just as immoral as the original bad act.

When we stand up for the rights of groups other than our own, we invite reciprocity. And when we treat others with disrespect, we invite reciprocity as well. Every person who quietly goes along with or benefits from prejudice is responsible for that prejudice. It's one of those areas where every decent person has an obligation to speak out.

Once a person has been taught to hate, it's very difficult to learn another way. But teaching can bring us beyond prejudice, and the best way to teach is by example. That means doing some basic things, like following "The Golden Rule." And it means confronting all of the prejudices that we're privy to in our daily lives.

For example, each of us should confront expressions of bigotry that we hear from family members, business associates, and friends.

Language shapes attitudes and conduct, and no slur should pass unchallenged. That's an important component of fighting prejudice; a step that each of us is equipped to take. And it's particularly important that we make it clear to children that we won't tolerate even offhanded expressions of bigotry from them or from others in our presence.

Confront the bigots. Shun their message. And deliver a message of your own: "It's fine to build yourself up, but don't tear other people down."

For example, don't say, "This is my religion, so it's the only one that's good." Say, "I'm glad you like your religion; I like mine too." And if a "religious" person voices a message of hate, ask, "Does your religion teach you to love people? Who does it teach you to love? Where in your holy scriptures does it teach bigotry and hate?"

In sum, each of us has to accept differences in others, and all of us should look for qualities in others that we can embrace. We must recognize that often there are different ways to be right, and sometimes there's no

> *I wish people would love everybody else the way they love me.*
> *It would be a better world.*
>
> MUHAMMAD ALI

absolute right or wrong.

All of us think that our beliefs are correct. Obviously, if we didn't, we'd believe something else. But when we were younger, we also believed in the correctness of our thoughts. And we know now that we weren't right about everything when we were young — nor are we now.

In the end then, the world becomes a better place to live each time someone embraces a philosophy of caring for all people, not just "one's own." That's one of the reasons that Martin Luther King, Jr. was truly great. The 1960s represented the height of the civil rights movement in the United States. Enormous progress was being made, but enormous risks lay ahead. The movement was in danger of being derailed. And just when that risk seemed greatest, Dr. King announced his opposition to the war in Vietnam. Many of his advisors counseled against that stand. They feared that his opposition to the war would be perceived as "unpatriotic," and that the entire civil rights movement would be undermined. But Dr. King adhered to the view that Vietnamese lives were just as sacred as the lives of black Americans. Even though the sojourn of his own ancestors in the United States had been long and bitter, he still had room in his heart for those of a different religion and color who lived halfway around the world. To Martin Luther King, Jr., all people were "his people." And it was a privilege to live in his time.

But it would be a mistake to think that bigotry and prejudice can be eradicated by deeds and words from leaders above. Tolerance and understanding won't "trickle down" in our society any more than wealth does. And if today's world is to be truly healed, that healing must be achieved one person at a time. The tolerance and understanding necessary to heal must come from each and every one of us, arising out of our everyday conduct, until decency reaches a flood tide.

Have we not all one father? Hath not one God created us all?

THE OLD TESTAMENT

BOOK OF MALACHI, CH. 2, VERSE 10

Let there be no compulsion in religion,

as truth stands out clear from error.

Whoever rejects evil and believes in God has grasped the most

trustworthy handhold that never breaks, and God hears and knows.

THE HOLY QUR'AN

SECOND SURA, VERSE 256

He who comes to a conclusion when the other side is unheard

may have been just in his conclusion, but has not been just in his conduct.

SENECA

Hate as though some day you will have to love.

ARISTOTLE

To escape hatred is to triumph.

CICERO

The Bounties of thy Lord

Are not closed to anyone

Those who believe in the Qur'an

Those who follow the Jewish scriptures

And the Sabians and the Christians

Any who believe in God

And the Last Day

And work righteousness

On them shall be no fear

Nor shall they grieve

HOLY QUR'AN

SEVENTEENTH SURA, VERSE 20

FIFTH SURA, VERSE 69

If a man say, "I love God," and hateth his neighbor, he is a liar.

THE NEW TESTAMENT

FIRST EPISTLE OF JOHN, CH. 4, VERSE 20

We have just enough religion to make us hate,
but not enough to make us love one another.

JONATHAN SWIFT

No one should try to pressure another person into
accepting a religion they don't want.

MUHAMMAD ALI

Prejudice is the reasoning of the stupid.

VOLTAIRE

I tolerate with the utmost latitude the right of others

to differ from me in opinion. I know too well the weakness and uncertainty

of human reason to wonder at its different results.

THOMAS JEFFERSON

No man is an island entire of itself.

Every man is a piece of the continent; a part of the main.

If a clod be washed away by the sea,

Europe is the lesser as well as if a promontory were;

as well as if a manor of thy friends or of thine own were.

Any man's death diminishes me, because I am involved in mankind.

Therefore, never send to know for whom the bell tolls.

It tolls for thee.

JOHN DONNE

Bigotry murders religion to frighten fools with her ghost.

C. C. COLTON

Let me never fall into the vulgar mistake of dreaming that
I am persecuted whenever I am contradicted.

RALPH WALDO EMERSON

If a man does not keep pace with his companions,

perhaps it is because he hears a different drummer.

Let him step to the music he hears,

however measured or far away.

HENRY DAVID THOREAU

Everything that I understand, I understand only because I love.

LEO TOLSTOY

One should examine oneself for a very long time before

thinking of condemning others.

MOLIÈRE

I was born on this earth,

so I come from the same womb as humans in all countries,

even though our body types may be different.

K'ANG YU-WEI

Whoever degrades another degrades me.

WALT WHITMAN

All religions must be tolerated,

for every man must be saved in his own way.

FREDERICK THE GREAT

There is no good result when hatred is returned for hatred.

JOHANN FRIEDRICH VON SCHILLER

Rulers ought to employ a page to repeat to them every morning:

"See that you do not extend

the power of the sword to touch the conscience."

JOSEPH GLANVILLE

A true man hates no one.

NAPOLEON I

If it be an evil to judge rashly or untruly any single man,
how much greater a sin it is to condemn a whole people.

WILLIAM   PENN

All bigotries hang to one another.

THOMAS JEFFERSON

If you want to understand others, look into your own heart.

JOHANN FRIEDRICH VON SCHILLER

Hate is fear, and fear is rot.

ROBERT GRAVES

Toleration is good for all or it is good for none.

EDMUND BURKE

To be prejudiced is always to be weak.

SAMUEL JOHNSON

Prejudice is the child of ignorance.

WILLIAM HAZLITT

The prejudice against color of which we hear so much

is no stronger than that against women.

It is produced by the same cause,

and manifested very much in the same way.

The Negro's skin and the woman's sex

are both prima facie evidence that they were intended

to be in subjection to the white Saxon man.

ELIZABETH CADY STANTON

At the heart of racism is the religious assertion that

God made a creative mistake

when He brought some people into being.

FRIEDRICH VON OTTO

Man's best candle is his understanding.

JAMES HOWELL

It is never too late to give up our prejudices.

HENRY DAVID THOREAU

Error of opinion may be tolerated where reason

is left free to combat it.

THOMAS JEFFERSON

History records the tragic fact that

men have gone to war and cut each other's throats

because they could not agree as to what

was to become of them after their throats were cut.

WALTER PARKER STACY

The mind of the bigot is like the pupil of the eye.

The more light you pour upon it,

the more it will contract.

OLIVER WENDELL HOLMES, JR.

Hate and mistrust are the children of blindness.

WILLIAM WATSON

All I care to know is that a man is a human being. That is enough for me.

The doctrine which from the very first has been held by bigots

of all sects when stripped of rhetorical disguise is simply this:

"I am in the right, and you are in the wrong.

When you are the stronger, you ought to tolerate me

for it is your duty to tolerate truth. But when I am the stronger,

I shall persecute you for it is my duty to persecute error."

THOMAS BABINGTON MACAULAY

Hatred is heavier freight for the shipper than it is for the consignee.

AUGUSTUS THOMAS

Hatred is the coward's revenge.

GEORGE BERNARD SHAW

To understand everything makes one tolerant.

GERMAINE BARONNE DESTAEL-HOLSTEIN

You can't spell "brothers" without including "others."

ANONYMOUS

All people serve the same God.
We just serve him in different ways.

MUHAMMAD ALI

The universal brotherhood of man—
what there is of it—is our most precious possession.

MARK TWAIN

If my theory of relativity is proven correct,

Germany will claim me as a German,

and France will declare that I am a citizen of the world.

Should my theory prove untrue,

France will say I am a German,

and Germany will declare that I am a Jew.

ALBERT EINSTEIN

I know of no rights of race superior to the rights of humanity.

FREDERICK DOUGLAS

Race prejudice decreases values; both real estate and human.

W. E. B. DUBOIS

The motto should not be, "Forgive one another."

Rather, it should be, "Understand one another."

EMMA GOLDMAN

It is easy to be tolerant when you do not care.

CLEMENT ROGERS

Whenever someone speaks with prejudice against a group —

Catholics, Jews, Italians, Negroes — someone else usually

comes up with a classic line of defense —

"Look at Einstein! Look at Carver! Look at Toscanini!"

So, of course, Catholics or Jews or Italians or Negroes must be all right.

These defenders mean well, but their approach is wrong.

What a minority group wants is not the right

to have geniuses among them, but the right to have fools and

scoundrels without being condemned as a group.

AGNES ELIZABETH BENEDICT

No loss by flood and lightning,

no destruction of cities and temples by the hostile forces of nature,

has deprived man of so many noble lives and impulses

as those which his intolerance has destroyed.

HELEN KELLER

Hatred is like fire; it makes even light rubbish deadly.

GEORGE ELIOT

Any man who tries to excite class hatred, sectional hate,

hate of creeds, any kind of hatred in our community,

though he may affect to do it in the interest of the class he is addressing,

is in the long run with absolute certainty that class's own worst enemy.

THEODORE ROOSEVELT

Whoever seeks to set one nationality against another seeks

to degrade all nationalities. Whoever seeks to set one race against

another seeks to enslave all races. Whoever seeks to set one religion

against another seeks to destroy all religion.

FRANKLIN ROOSEVELT

All progress begins with differences of opinion

and moves onward as the differences are adjusted through

reason and mutual understanding.

HARRY TRUMAN

No one can make you feel inferior without your consent.

Love your enemies. It makes them so damn mad.

P. D. EAST

I want, by understanding myself, to understand others.

I want to be all that I am capable of becoming.

KATHERINE MANSFIELD

Hatred floods your mind with the idea of the one you hate.

Your thoughts reflect his, and you act in his spirit.

If you wish to be like your enemy, to be wholly his, hate him.

CHARLES HORTON COOLEY

He who will not reason is a bigot.

He who cannot reason is a fool.

And he who dares not reason is a slave.

WILLIAM DRUMMOND

You lose a lot of time hating people.

MARIAN ANDERSON

It is a good thing to demand liberty for ourselves and

for those who agree with us. But it is a better thing and a rarer thing

to give liberty to others who do not agree with us.

FRANKLIN ROOSEVELT

No people on earth can be held, as a people, to be an enemy, for all

humanity shares the common hunger for peace and fellowship and justice.

DWIGHT EISENHOWER

Persecution, whenever it occurs,

establishes only the power and cunning of the persecutor,

not the truth and worth of his belief.

H. M. KALLEN

A sensible human being always learns more from his opponents

than from his fervent supporters.

WALTER LIPPMANN

Since when do you have to agree with people to defend them from injustice?

LILLIAN HELLMAN

Understanding is a two-way street.

ELEANOR ROOSEVELT

No man has ever been born a Negro hater,

a Jew hater, or any other kind of hater.

Nature refuses to be involved in such suicidal practices.

HARRY BRIDGES

Love lights more fires than hate extinguishes.

ELLA WILCOX

Folks never understand the folks they hate.

JAMES RUSSELL LOWELL

No person is strong enough to carry a cross

and a prejudice at the same time.

WILLIAM WARD

You cannot conquer the world for the God of love by a jihad of hate.

M .   S .   L A Z A R O N

Tolerance is giving to every other human being

every right that you claim for yourself.

ROBERT INGERSOLL

A man who lives not by what he loves but

by what he hates is a sick man.

ARCHIBALD MACLEISH

Whoever kindles the flames of intolerance is lighting

a fire underneath his own home.

HAROLD STASSEN

There is but one race — humanity.

GEORGE MOORE

The highest result of education is tolerance.

HELEN KELLER

We must either learn to live together as brothers
or we are all going to perish together as fools.

MARTIN LUTHER KING, JR.

When you harm and mistreat other people,
that's disrespecting God, who created them.

MUHAMMAD ALI

There are no "white" or "colored" signs on the graveyards of battle.

JOHN F. KENNEDY

If we really want human brotherhood to spread and

increase until it makes life safe and sane,

we must also be certain that there is no one true faith

or path by which it may spread.

ADLAI STEVENSON

Hate is rooted in fear.

But hatred and bitterness can never cure the disease of fear.

Only love can do that. Hatred paralyzes life;

love releases it. Hatred confuses life;

love harmonizes it. Hatred darkens life; love illuminates it.

MARTIN LUTHER KING, JR.

In the end, as any successful teacher will tell you,

you can only teach the things that you are.

If we practice racism, then it is racism that we teach.

MAX LERNER

You cannot shake hands with a clenched fist.

INDIRA GANDHI

One night, I lay awake amid sleeping Muslim brothers.

And I learned that pilgrims from every land,

every color and class and rank, all snored in the same language.

MALCOLM X

If you really believe in the brotherhood of man and

want to come into its fold, you've got to let everyone else in too.

OSCAR HAMMERSTEIN

Without brotherhood, peace is not possible.

FAITH BALDWIN

Race prejudice is not only a shadow over the colored.

It is a shadow over all of us,

and the shadow is darkest over those who feel it least

and allow its evil effects to go on.

PEARL BUCK

I think I have discovered the highest good.
It is love. Love is the most durable power in the world.

MARTIN LUTHER KING, JR.

The rights of all men are threatened

when the rights of any man are threatened.

JOHN F. KENNEDY

If we were to wake up some morning and find that

everyone was the same race, creed, and color,

we would find some other causes for prejudice before noon.

GEORGE AIKEN

What are little hates but little deaths that wander on and on.

WALTER GREENOUGH

An aggressor will someday die,

but the act of aggression remains forever.

May we turn it into a remembrance in human consciousness,

so that it is not to be repeated.

IBRAHIM M. OWEISS

The price of hating other human beings is loving oneself less.

ELDRIDGE CLEAVER

*Our Jewish friends have demonstrated their commitment
to the principles of tolerance and brotherhood in many ways and
often at great personal sacrifice. Can we ever express our
appreciation to the rabbis who chose to give moral witness with us?
And who can ever forget the sacrifice of two Jewish lives,
Andrew Goodman and Michael Schwerner, in the swamps of Mississippi?
It would be impossible to record the contribution
that the Jewish people have made toward
the Negro's struggle for freedom — it has been so great.*

MARTIN LUTHER KING, JR.

The world is white no longer, and it will never be again.

JAMES BALDWIN

*Hate is able to provoke disorders, to ruin a social organization,
to cast a country into bloody revolution; but it produces nothing.*

GEORGES SOREL

We all inhabit this small planet. We all breathe the same air.
We all cherish our children's future. And we are all mortal.

JOHN F. KENNEDY

To strike the chains of a slave is noble.

To leave him the captive of the color of his skin is hypocrisy.

While we in America have freed the slave of his chains,

we have not freed his heirs of their color.

Until justice is blind to color,

until education is unaware of race,

until opportunity ceases to squint its eyes at

pigmentation of human complexions,

emancipation will be a proclamation — but it will not be a fact.

LYNDON JOHNSON

Hatred leads to the extinction of values.

JOSE ORTEGA Y'GASSET

The real problem of our existence lies in the fact

that we ought to love one another but do not.

REINHOLD NIEBUHR

He who hates does not know God.

MARTIN LUTHER KING, JR.

In the past, yes, I have made sweeping indictments of all white people.

I will never be guilty of that again,

as I know now that some white people are truly sincere,

that some truly are capable of being brotherly toward a black man.

The true Islam has shown me that a blanket indictment

of all white people is as wrong as

when whites make blanket indictments against blacks.

MALCOLM X

I imagine one of the reasons people cling to

their hates so stubbornly is because they sense, once hate is gone,

they will be forced to deal with pain.

JAMES BALDWIN

I've seen too much hate to want to hate myself.

Every time I see it, I say to myself, hate is too great a burden to bear.

MARTIN LUTHER KING, JR.

Let racism be a problem to someone else. Let it drag them down.
Don't use it as an excuse for your own shortcomings.

COLIN POWELL

There is something that I must say to my people who stand

on the warm threshold which leads into the palace of justice.

In the process of gaining our rightful place,

we must not be guilty of wrongful deeds.

Let us not seek to satisfy our thirst for freedom by

drinking from the cup of bitterness and hatred.

MARTIN LUTHER KING, JR.

Let us not be blind to our differences.

But let us direct attention to our common interests and

help make the world safe for diversity.

JOHN F. KENNEDY

I have learned that whenever a single human being is humiliated,

the human image is cheapened.

ELIE WIESEL

*I remember the year that Muhammad telephoned to wish me
a Merry Christmas. Think about that. A Muslim calling a Jew
to wish him well on a Christian holiday.
There's a message in that for anyone who's listening.*

THOMAS HAUSER

Life is short, we get old so fast.
It doesn't make sense to waste time on hating.

MUHAMMAD ALI